**This book is to be returned on or before
the last date stamped below.**

Education Services

Falkirk Council

Over the Moon

A Book of Sayings

Over the Moon

A Book of Sayings
chosen and illustrated by
Shirley Hughes

faber and faber

First published in 1980
This edition first published in 1998
by Faber and Faber Limited
3 Queen Square London WC1N 3AU

Typeset by Faber and Faber Ltd
Printed in England by Clays Ltd, St Ives plc

Shirley Hughes is hereby identified as author of this
work in accordance with Section 77 of the Copyright,
Designs and Patents Act 1988

A CIP record for this book
is available from the British Library

ISBN 0–571–19438–9

2 4 6 8 10 9 7 5 3 1

Introduction

Sayings are a wonderful ornament to our spoken language. In one sense, they are a kind of theatre of the absurd. Children, hearing them dropped into the adult conversation, form indestructible pictures in the head. What could be more intriguing than the thought of the sky raining cats and dogs, or a skeleton in the cupboard, or a bull let loose in a china shop? The true meanings of these metaphors often dawn much later.

As with nursery rhymes, they are an unmissable part of an English-speaking childhood no matter what ethnic background we may come from. The fun of illustrating this book has been in putting the literal image alongside a simple explanation of the meaning.

Shirley Hughes

Contents

Raining cats and dogs

Raining very hard

Tied to his mother's apron strings

Completely controlled by his mother

Teaching your grandmother how to suck eggs

Telling people how to do something when they know more
about it than you do

3

Toeing the line

Having to behave like everyone else

Minding your p's and q's

Being specially careful to behave well

As though he'd been pulled through a
hedge backwards

Very messy and untidy

Being a dog in the manger

Refusing to give up something you don't really want to someone who needs it

Up a gum tree

Trapped in an impossible position

7

Down the drain

Wasted and done for

Up the spout

*Finished – there's
nothing more to be done*

A flea in her ear

A telling-off

8

In a tight corner

In a really difficult position, one that's going to be hard to get out of

Not pulling your punches

Honest straight talking

Playing with fire

*Messing about with something that might become
really dangerous*

Up the creek without a paddle

In a hopeless state

Looking for a needle in a haystack

Doing something impossible

A skeleton in the cupboard

Something you'd very much rather no one knew about

15

The last straw that broke the camel's back

*The one last trouble that makes everything
impossible to bear*

As thick as thieves

Best friends, or people who see a great deal of each other

Taking pot luck

Putting up with what is offered

A bull in a china shop

Thoughtlessly clumsy and destructive

19

Like a cat that's got the cream

Smug and self-satisfied

Like a dog with two tails

Very pleased with yourself

Keeping your nose to the grindstone

Keeping hard at work

Hitting the nail on the head

Giving exactly the right explanation

Swallowed hook, line and sinker

Accepted without question

In at the deep end

Getting deeply involved at once

Over the moon

Extremely delighted

Putting the cat among the pigeons

Making mischief

Set a thief to catch a thief

A wrong-doer will be good at catching someone who is doing the same thing

Keep it under your hat

Keep this to yourself, as a secret between us

Cards on the table

Open and honest about your intentions

Leading her up the garden path

*Fooling someone by pretending to offer her something
which you don't mean to give*

Forty winks

A short nap

Shutting the stable door after the horse has bolted

Taking precautions when it's already too late

Sitting on the fence

Refusing to take sides

Casting pearls before swine

Offering your best to someone who can't appreciate it

This won't buy the baby a new
bonnet

This won't get us anywhere

Tighten your belt

Make do with less

Like a bear with a sore head

Very cross indeed

A chip off the old block

Taking after his Dad

Like a cat on hot bricks

Nervous and jumpy

When my ship comes home

When I'm rich enough to have and do all the things I dream of

36

Turning a blind eye

Pretending not to notice something you'd rather wasn't there

Pulling the wool over his eyes

Deceiving him

Born with a silver spoon in his
mouth

*Born into a wealthy family, with
every advantage*

As dead as a dodo

*Absolutely finished and over with
(a dodo is an extinct bird)*